GOING TO THE EYESTONE

GOING TO THE EYESTONE

Deirdre Diana Dwyer

Wolsak and Wynn . Toronto

© Deirdre Diana Dwyer 2002

All rights reserved. No part of this book may be reproduced or transmitted in any form, by any means, electronic or mechanical, without permission in writing from the publisher, except by a reviewer, who may quote brief passages in a review. In case of photocopying or other reprographic copying, a licence is required from CANCOPY (Canadian Copyright Licensing Agency), One Yonge Street, Suite 1900, Toronto, Ontario, Canada M5E 1E5.

Typeset in Meta
Printed in Canada by The Coach House Printing Company, Toronto.
Cover design: The Coach House Printing Company, Toronto
Author's photograph: © Eleonore Schonmaier

Some of the poems included in this book have, appeared or will appear in *The Antigonish Review, ARC, The Bourbon St. Workshop/Ecphore Instalation* [sic] *Piece, CVII, The Dalhousie Review,The Fiddlehead, The Gaspereau Review, Grail, Grain, Meltwater, The New Quarterly, The Pottersfield Portfolio, TickleAce, The White Wall Review, The Windsor Review, Writer's Block Magazine, Zygote.*

The publisher thanks the
Canada Council for the Arts
and the Ontario Arts Council
for their generous support.

The Canada Council for the Arts | Le Conseil des Arts du Canada

ONTARIO ARTS COUNCIL
CONSEIL DES ARTS DE L'ONTARIO

Wolsak and Wynn Publishers Ltd
192 Spadina Avenue, Suite 315
Toronto, Ontario
Canada M5T 2C2

National Library of Canada Cataloguing in Publication Data
Deirdre Diane Dwyer, 1958-
      Going to the Eyestone
Poems.
ISBN 0-919897-83-5

I. Title

PS8557.W93G63 2002   C811'.54   C2002-901058-6
PR9199.3.D895G63 2002

*For my parents, brothers, and sisters,
who helped when the splinters were sharp*

*For Dana, Amy and Anna Kittilsen, and Kevin,
Christopher and Patrick Dwyer, who are a-going*

And for Hans, because we are a-going too.

Contents

1 SPLINTERS

The strangers we are -11
Fragments, the 1917 Halifax Explosion -13
Drawing wild animals -16
The photograph -18
Gwlladys -20
Projections -22
What might make us whole -26
Family -27
We gather in public places -28
Moir's Island -29
That time of month -30
The telephone, five studies -31
This time last year -33
Streetlights and shadow -35
When there isn't much to say -36
The last time -37
And the flowers grow regardless -38
A gift of tears -39
When sleep comes -41
The sea or salvation -44

2 THE GOING

Waiting for the storm -47
The print on the wall -48
Scraps -49
Skating over the moment -51
The book of dreams -52
At the centre of things -53
Looking at a photograph of my parents -54
The sun all day -55

Tubing festival, Gaspereau   -57
Fuchsias, long distance   -58
The dishes so slowly   -60
The lights behind me   -61
What he will teach us   -63
The careful path back to naïve   -65
Island going   -67
The blue egg   -68
When we turn around   -70
Rooms for yourself   -72
The photographer   -73

3 THE EYESTONE

The day you saw the world   -77
The auction at day's end   -79
Mornings by the water   -80
Again   -82
You want to interview angels   -83
Hand-mirror   -84
The day the bookmobile came   -85
After "Collected Landscapes"   -87
Reading in the bath   -88
At the rapids   -90
Legend   -91
Gratitude, from the clam factory   -92
On the path to the waterfall   -93

1 SPLINTERS

We have now seen two eyestones in Cape Breton—an item so rare and so long out of use it seems no longer to be remembered in Scotland, the place from which both of the eyestones came. John Tom Urquhart of Skir Dhu first told us of the eyestone. Later, we met John A. Wilkie of Sugar Loaf. He showed us his eyestone and told a story almost identical to the story John Tom told.

The eyestone was not originally found in Scotland. They seem all to have come there from the Far East. They are the colour of flesh and about the size of half a pea. And they are said to be the tip of a conch shell. The eyestone is alive, and has to eat—and both men keep theirs in about an inch and a half of sugar (John Tom uses white sugar; John A. uses brown). John Tom sometimes feeds his a little rum, and he changes the sugar every two or three years. When the first Highland settlers came to Cape Breton, they brought the eyestone with them. It was . . . passed along from father to son.

John Tom said that the eyestone would be used to get a splinter out of a man's eye. Years ago, when it was common for men to work with chisels and hammers and sledges, men often caught a speck of steel in the eye. John A. said that the eyestone could retrieve other things as well. He said, "I was sawing wood at Bay St. Laurence. I got sawdust in my eye, and in the evening it got to be sore—it got so bad the other eye was getting sore. And they said to me, 'You better go to where the eyestone is tonight.'"

[So that it will not be lost] you go to the eyestone and it rarely travels . . .

"Years ago," said John A., "there was a man who wanted to say how awful a certain woman was, so he said of her she was so mean she wouldn't feed the eyestone."

—Down North: The Book of Cape Breton's Magazine

THE STRANGERS WE ARE

My best friend in grade seven
was one of those kids,
children of fishermen,
who brought milk to school in Mason jars,
when there was nothing better
brought lobster sandwiches for lunch
and were ashamed.

I remember staying overnight at her house,
the kitchen always smelling
of boiled cabbage, corned beef
and rubber boots in the front hall.
The two of us in her bedroom
perched on the edge of our beds
looking at each other
not knowing what to do with ourselves.
How I pretended not to be scared
by the strangers we were
in a new setting.

Outside, beyond the few small houses
the government wharf
with its boats,
their bellies slick with bright paint.

Boats sad at their inactivity.
The wind knocking them against the dock
speaking to that uselessness
just as a tractor parked in a field
is lonely, and a grown woman
alone with her father
doesn't know what to say.

In grade ten when I don't
know her any more my friend
will be the girl who got pregnant that year.
She'll leave school and her parents

will raise the child that everyone
is supposed to know
as her youngest brother.

Every school year had one birth and one death.
Grade twelve: a boy drowned
in a canoe accident.
I remember the day it happened,
the dense fog of the morning.
Under his yearbook photo I read
   to everything there is a season
but I don't believe it.

There are people
who want to make you believe it,
though they can't tell you why.
     You're not sure
they even believe it themselves.

They just keep on
living with the answers they have.
Like women who carefully fill huge jars
full of buttons, who then have to stretch to return
those jars to the pantry's top shelf,
they know it's all a pretence
—there are scraps and loose ends.

We pretend our lives are useful and tidy,
that we're not strangers
to each other in our houses,
that we are not scared
of those questions
that shake you and put you back down
rearranged.

FRAGMENTS, THE 1917 HALIFAX EXPLOSION

What we don't know is splinters and glass
in our hands. Think of the school children,
a historian in a basement archive
sorting through their unclaimed belongings,
opening a mildewed notebook,
a ten-year-old's
long division problems

>How many dead? how many
>without limbs or blind?

opening another notebook,
reading the first spelling list:

>*thou, eternity, away, forever ...*

closing the book
to stare into the large space
that those words unlock.

Think of a shiver, an explosion
in the body—travelling up the spine
as if it travels through time,
the force, echoing in you,
that shattered so much of the city.

Think of my grandparents that December morning,
two young people, who don't know
each other, in different parts of the city,
the only pieces of the story I have
and they will tell only a part of it:

that in a convent classroom
books fell off the edge of her desk,

that he turned over in his sleep and dreamt
the silence at the eye of a storm,
to which his alarm clock surrendered ...
when he should have been waiting for a train.

Think of children standing in windows
dazzled by ships in the harbour;

in the same way we turn our faces
to the sun, close our satisfied eyes.

What about the grown-ups
who should have been wary if they weren't
terrified of the ships' awful cargo.

            Think of what happened next—
            windows breaking thirty miles outside the city,
            his train station in acres of rubble.

And of what hasn't been told—these clean wounds
like the girl in a photograph of the class of 1917.
            She's up to her neck in history!
You can tell her face is turned to the camera
by how she sits at her desk, but the face itself
is a blur, an overexposure of light
or of time as if she suffers the price for staring into the future.

Who is blinded here?
Not my grandmother who rose from her desk
to collect her books
before her chair was pierced with glass.

She's safe
though a policeman stood perplexed
at the door when he asked about the girls
and was told   They're in Eden.
What else would nuns name their garden!

My grandfather safe too,
saved by the silence of a clock
that kept him away from the station,
the North End's flat landscape of forever.

My grandparents can meet and marry now.
Give them a few years.

DRAWING WILD ANIMALS

I remember when Uncle Fred came to visit
he helped us draw elephants
on one of those mechanical toys:
turn it over and the drawing disappears.

Turn it over, turn over the stories of family,
trying to understand them
and lacy patterns you made all over the page
with your Spirograph.

So many questions dressed up
to look like someone you know.

                        Simple questions
like why he lived in Florida.
I thought family was like colouring:
you're not allowed to go outside the lines.

Even family saints have their skeletons:
my mother mentioned Sonia, his wife.

                He has to take care of her.

I imagine her in a warm room, the windows
wide open, the air conditioner
doesn't work, Sonia's hair is sizzled and teased,
her every movement nervous.
Her eyes see your aura.

When Fred appeared again
I studied him, looking for signs
of her. I did not ask him
to draw animals from foreign countries.

And I remember the story of Fred's son:
Barry handsome like his father,
but enough of Sonia in him
that he tried to see everything.

Sketch the story of Barry
going behind the barn
with a gun. Turn the picture
over—

THE PHOTOGRAPH

When she was eighty-two,
I found in my grandmother's desk
a photograph of her
        how many years younger?
standing on a verandah
beside her husband,
their hands almost meeting
on an empty wooden lawn chair.

He wears a three-piece suit
and she, squinting into the sun,
also wears formal dress.
They look uncomfortable
with themselves, their faces
not letting go of a darkness
the sun wants to spoil.

Behind them: the end
of a field, a narrow stretch of beach
that makes way for water,
the complete white of the sky.

Were they happy? Did they love
how they dealt with those things unexpected,
the choices they made? That weekend
at the cottage—did she want to be alone
with her husband, to ask him how much he cared
when my parents arrived, uninvited
and they had to practice civility.
When someone wanted a photo
they all went out to the deck.

Maybe my grandmother wanted to talk
to another woman—my mother
being the only one close by—
wanting to ask her about romance,
and compromise.

Maybe she knew
she couldn't ask anyone this.

How we assume two people
overlap, are more than their bodies,
carry between them a tray
of things that make a marriage.

I remember an English teacher
in high school telling us
secrets from the future,
my moving to the edge of my seat
away from grammar, parts of speech—

    why was he telling us this?

—that the way we love our parents will change.

His open disclosure so matter-of-fact
I believed him completely,
though I had no real reason to.
I could not even define the love,
like a house I walked around in;
couldn't, then, see beyond
the bright orbit of adolescence.

My grandparents' hands almost meeting
on an empty wooden lawn chair,
maybe they are standing there
waiting for the future to walk in
and sit down
and say

    you can love now
    is that what you want?

GWLLADYS

You were the *other* grandmother,
the one who pecked at our cheeks,
the one with a Welsh name that keeps
company with *Gertrude* and *Myrtle*,
uglier for a name that brayed at us
when we talked of you.

You were *other*,
married your sister's widower—
did you feel you were second choice?
did you marry for the sake of his daughter?
: my mother years later,
who later still went to your house
every day, delivering groceries, some kind
of dependency—call it *family*, I guess,
as the two of you bickered all the while.

Our crone with the spinning wheel.

At Christmas, birthdays we took the path
to your house, the shortcut under the pines
to the gravelled drive. Our reluctant conversation
in the sun porch surrounded by
coloured glass bottles, books, ceramic jars.

We went home eagerly,
happy with our envelopes,
your sprawling signature
beneath a clean bill.

Older, our conversations longer.
My mother returned with leftovers of food
and argument. You offered drinks
at Christmas, walked slowly
not only with weight; we tried to overlook
diseased bruises on your leg.

Then you were other again
dying six months after my father's mother.
My mother relieved, I found myself
thinking about how we made you
other, the silence you kept with my father
that we did not question
                              —or could not—

trusting incoherent accounts
of conflict and deceit, the sharp
hard-to-find edges of family history,
thinking about your last will and testament,
Gwlladys, this thin testament,
and what we pass on
to our survivors.

Projections

1

   Play the movie backwards
       we cried
and we watched ourselves
take up the Christmas gift
we had just laid down, that gesture like a promise.
We watched ourselves walk backwards
away from the tree to the kitchen,
into the past holding
the future in our hands,
the future all wrapped up.

   Again! we cheered
from one end of the darkened room.
Behind the projector's
aurora borealis of dust, we saw
ourselves grow younger

each time hoping
the camera would show us more
of its strange magic and keep on rolling,
transporting us to a time when our parents
didn't know the full flesh of the word *child*,
long before we were more awkward
than awkward.

2
What I remember of the years
when the house was crowded,
full of the five of us—call us siblings
but the word hisses
like the witch who wanted us
off of her land.

   Go back, she shrieked,
   where you came from.

3
                    Go further back, says another voice.

To John, the first-born, at four
feeding ducks in the Public Gardens,
wearing a little-boy blazer, shorts, a bow tie.

Or, a few years older, a suede jacket
with Davy Crockett fringes. He marches
miniature armies onto the beach,

sinks down into a trench—
you see only the plastic oak leaves
on his helmet.

More than a few battles later,
I walk out of his office where he explains
geological charts, the shifting lines, the faults.

He proposed, his wife told me, when
out driving—they stopped, she thought,
for just another rock formation,
not one clear, hard stone.

4
Kay and I are walking to school,
passing the brook that in the spring
fills with gaspereaux. She says
                "you're walking too fast"
But she always says that.

Perhaps I wanted to walk out of that time
into a future I thought would be brighter.
                            And was it?

Sometimes.
Like lightning that cuts through a darkness,

before it sets fire to a tree.
We fought—pulled hair, scratched,
kicked each other in the shins,
were fighting our inextricable bond.

5
To find the boys' room
walk up the stairs, turn right—
you'll hear Ian at night before
you see him, laughing, being tickled.

Before you hear the story of Ian
taking scissors to sheets drying in the basement.

Or the story of Ian jumping ice cakes
until one drifted too far,
Mom teaching him a lesson,
telling him to wade to shore.

The story of Ian and local geography:
                What river is this?
as we drive up the Musquodoboit valley
crossing Yes the same river
under so many bridges.

6
Because Ann was too young to remember
the home movies, the bulky pale brown
projector, the grainy image of us walking
backwards into the kitchen
            if she's told *Go back!*

              she won't know
where to go. What images can she hold onto?
She can't even remember the time she "ran away"
trying to visit her friend she thought
lived right next door.

Ann, like us, too young
to know the word distance
which keeps whispering to us,
                      Go back

because it wanted to see
the gifts before they were opened.

WHAT MIGHT MAKE US WHOLE

November clouds stampeding across the sky,
we followed my older brother for answers,
for questions, and secrets like old trees,
gnarled and solid.

What might make us older?—our questions,
wind chasing the grass of a dark field—
                              cigarettes?
in coded teenage words.

The Old Mine's Road where I picked blueberries
was more than its name too, was going double on bikes
to get there, someone telling me how
babies were made:
                rubbing, she said
and I didn't want to believe her.

Even in the country things break
—secret gardens, moss pulled from forest floors,
the branches of birch trees
laden with snow.

Later we followed the boys to the Puffa-puffa shack
—we wouldn't guess their hiding place?

My brother reluctantly patient with us
as we choked on what we thought
would make us older—smoke
as our lungs pulled that secret in
and we exhaled.

FAMILY

In my parents' house,
alone, I could finally hear
the stunning quiet of the rooms,
the clock on the mantle promising
a new future every second

but how could I find it when
it was shapeless and fluid?
                             I rummaged
for my parents' true story
and mine

as if I thought they would leave them
behind, as if there are things so fine-grained
we lose them among the debris.

I pulled out the weighted top drawer
of my mother's dresser
full of nail polish, foundation, eye shadows
she seldom used. I pushed it shut

reassured, somehow, by wooden handles
shaped like scallop shells. I meandered
through the house, churning
stubborn details: photographs, books,
the empty rooms

                 and family, that crowd
of push and pull me,
who could only bring me those solid things
I could name

           like this privacy
which is a kind of love.

We Gather in Public Places

We enter the hall, gather together
the folds, the muted plaid of private moments.
Dropping the thick coat, what has been our life,
we shake off sleepiness, one sleeve.

We shake it off and down,
pretending we recognise the cloth
we find beneath, the many layers.
Using the language of cats,
we won't confess the inelegance of a fall

though we shift in our seats
like a bear going around
and around in its bed,
trying to settle in for the winter.

We sniff the air discreetly, for enemies,
trade tentative watchwords.

Our talk drifts, and falls
and rises; the birds of summer
scale the autumn wind.

We drop many layers, but still
there's a space around us
we won't take off
                              as we learn to be
one great new animal, a crowd.

Moir's Island

The mother Moir whistled like a bird
when she called her fourteen children home.
No mistaking the sound that travelled
across the inlet to our beach
where, all day, swimming and sand
were something
we breathed.

The causeway took them
back to the island where a statue of Mary presided
over a bush of poisonous red berries;
in her calm blue robe, she seemed to whisper
    Don't touch, don't eat
while St. Francis, like a lighthouse,
surveyed the sea. During the lonely winters
seagulls kept him company. There were rocks

around the island, treasure-rocks with red paint
to mark the spot where pirates once boasted
— there must have been pirates — we could not find
their secret hoards. Some summers
nuns in their habits and their hoods
would tread the causeway. We swam
or rowed, ate green apples,
played summer games in the grass, and drank
orange Kool-Aid until we were tired

and sick of orange Kool-Aid — could I
drink it now and not hear the *All's Well*
we cried from the rock we climbed upon,
the sound of teenagers swimming, laughing in the dark
at their nakedness, the sound of Whip-poor-will,
the mother Moir calling the children home? We heard
the tail of that call, the feather
that sounded so forlorn,
so much like loss.

THAT TIME OF MONTH

It's like watching rain showering
a distance away: gentle,
but somehow ominous;
you don't know how close that rain
will come to you.
It's like whales adding new notes
to their elegies,
the sound of loons laughing
over the sky behind you,
like changing your clothes seven times
and none of them know
the mood you're in.
You don't know yourself.
Like when you're walking to work in the morning,
coming out of the graveyard
you discover the gold-green sunlight
of early September.
Summer's just gone and the leaves can't decide
what colour to turn.
Like walking home from work:
the sky's a mess: one part blue,
one large cloud above the trees
is the colour of the second layer
of wallpaper: a muted brownish grey.
Another cloud the colour of sour milk
has its edges covered in gold leaf
by undistinguished sunlight.

THE TELEPHONE, FIVE STUDIES

1
"I'll call you," he said,
but he didn't and now as she dials,
she wonders if he loves another,
imagines him kissing someone
else, kisses that undress
her doubts, the woman
she could have been. She imagines his love
-making interrupted by the phone ringing. Maybe
he knows she's the one
calling by the urgency of the rings.
That's why he won't pick it up,
though he wants to hear the phone.
He craves the calls of many women
who know his passion
is notorious.

2
You listen to the ringing in that room
that's empty except for the last slice of pizza
in the box, the empty bottles of beer: they're outside,
unloading the truck, making jokes;
boxes in their arms, they think they have everything
they want, nothing they want to avoid
when they hear the phone,
the phone that's still ringing.

3
He moves the papers on his desk
to find the phone as he checks
the clock, wonders why his wife is late
for the meeting to discuss
their debts. He envisions his son grabbing
a pot of boiling water, oh and the boy screams,
or maybe his daughter drove her tricycle
off the curb. He hears the screech of brakes
and hopes … the phone still ringing.

4
She's sitting beside the phone
when it rings, but she doesn't
want to answer it
too soon. He'll think she's too eager
and that will sour the affair
—oh, will it be him? let it be—
before it begins. She knows
some people are susceptible,
and how others can hear eagerness
in its naïveté.

5
I count out five rings,
then maybe three more, giving
them time to get in the door,
to conjure a weak excuse,
to catch their breath,
or their heart.

In all those rooms
the telephone,
an instrument
of loneliness.

This Time Last Year

All day I felt I was missing something,
that I'd left something behind:
a toothbrush, a comb
or a mirror.

Rain all day, nothing extraordinary
until the radio reminded me
of our celebration: this time last year
you brought red wine to my house.
Sitting on the sofa at the window
we drank it under autumn trees
that entered the room
with their afternoon light.

This time last year I was
starting to touch the inside
of your denim-covered thigh.
I wanted to put down the wine glass
to kiss you. Before the bottle was empty
we probably left it on the living room floor.

But what time is it now?
Four o'clock, the better part of the afternoon
gone.   This time last year
you were leaving,
for supper with your wife.

I stood at the top of the stairs
and you kissed me goodbye.
You turned, said something, halfway down
—smiling the whole time—
about our potent red wine.
Then at the bottom of the stairs you started to turn—
                    but you can't or won't.
You continued on out the door
to your car and drove off.

I'm still at the top of the stairs
watching you, a nude man descending a staircase,
putting his clothes back on.

And I,
I am completely naked.

STREETLIGHT AND SHADOW

The soft shoulder of a candle leans
toward two women talking:
    "An artist I knew said
the snow in shadow is not white."
    "But what colour," I ask her, "isn't love?"

Late night and I phone
a man in another city. Our letters
like dictionaries in which
so many words are crossed out.

    In knowing me, he wrote,
    you must have seen these clouds before.

Late night, the whole sky
between us saying nothing.

But he says   *Come back.*

I don't want to listen when she urges
me to wait; shadows in a dark room
are not such a mystery. Even small words
expand under the scrutiny of the stars.
His thoughts may change
with newly painted walls.

But what he writes   *All I can say ...*
is really nothing at all.

Three a.m.,
if I go to the living room
I'll make sense of moonlight,
approaching dawn,
what the streetlights do
to a room with large windows.

When There Isn't Much to Say

What can we say when men fold up their hearts,
their paper hearts, like origami
but without the gentleness, the delicate folds
of kimono and rice paper
and still they say words like freedom and love
in the same sentence
believing they can't find one
in the other.

       They come and go
between phone calls,
the time between the calls increasing.
Meanwhile the summer flowers have died.
Asters line the roadside and goldenrod
looks like someone's hair
and paisley scarves.

I could have said that few good men
will love us for the length and breadth
of our lives. But you already know that.
Words are useless when the heart loses
its place, when one good man knows
he doesn't want to be
that place. Night and the walls are darker.
I can hear you crying when I'm not there.

THE LAST TIME

All my lost friends, lovers, housemates—
I saw you last: on the second floor of a row house
on Bishop Street where you were angry
in your quiet contained way
at a lover with his abrupt ending.
At a table in a Thai village
with your parents, where we talked about Lonely Planet,
villagers who thought everyone who wrote
worked for Lonely Planet.
Wringing out hand-washing under a lemon tree
on Samos where we unfolded our stories
like old sheets too long in a closet.
After the late movie I sat
in a silent living room while you
slept through our silences, two
sets of expectations until
I asked what we were all about
and we loved furiously in Fuji-city then.
In your apartment above the river: the flute
on the coffee table, maps in the entrance way
and geology between miso soup
and plans for work in the Arctic—
"What did you say?" you asked, distracted.
When we drank too much
in the snug outside Cork
—"Why not?" I asked, his answer was sinking
in, though we got along fine otherwise, laughed
even, did all the domestic things.
After making love, we stood outside
by the car with its frozen doors,
everyone in the house knowing
that this was the last time before I flew
off to another home and you
to your wife.

Indelible the ink of the last time
when it is or is not known for what it will be.

AND THE FLOWERS GROW REGARDLESS
in memory of Jacinthe Casaubon

All summer, Jacinthe, I wanted to say flowers,
wanted to say death lightly
to myself, to get used to it.
I wanted to say How are you?

nonchalantly at a party you attended
dressed in a red skirt, black velvet,
a scarf around your head.

How are you? I said meaning
more than I meant to, as we played birthday games,
scavenged for next year's calendars,
while the garden grew taller outside.

I wanted to say love, to send
a postcard when we went on holiday.
I should have written.

And after the nurse has gone,
they roll you over
to wash you in the bed
where the flowers are all cotton now.

"She's tired," her husband said, "She's sad
you have to go. Put her glasses on, so she'll know
who is saying goodbye."

And I say flowers and love
now, but did you know that? I ask,
the day you died, when you might
or might not have known.

A GIFT OF TEARS

A day when so much
                        breaks open,
so much of what I read brings me
to tears, a sudden gulf.

Henry James advising his nephew
"Three things in life are important."
He leans over the crib.
"The first is to be kind."
He throws a ball to the boy, now 5.
"The second is to be kind."
The boy, twenty now, asks what
he ought to do with his life,
how he ought to live.
"And the third" he says
—accumulated pools inside me flood—
"the third is to be kind!"

Or Heaney on the phone
waiting for the message conveyed, pulling
the sound of clocks in a hallway in
through the funnel of the phone.
"Next thing he spoke and I nearly said I loved him"
brought as Heaney was
to thoughts of weeds and leeks,
and Death.

Or Tess responding to the poem
her husband wrote. What he would never know
of her later years, how
he would never nurse her,
                        the sorry in that.

His "Summer Fog"
which I read to you, 2 a.m., in bed.
Oh poems aloud after love.
I read Tess writing of his "gift"
to her against the solitude to come—

                                        so much

poetry in her prose,
the life in the death
to come and the dying.

And tears that make me larger.

Or no, I did not cry them
but heard my voice
breaking on such pliancy and softness
as he passes her the poem,
       answers the call,
particular raspberries picked.

As I learn to read aloud the words,
feeling together as we are
so much of what will come.

WHEN SLEEP COMES
    in memory of Henry DeEll & Larry Lamont

1
When we fall back
the cushions are no longer there; it's hard
believing you're not alive—

death with its
hard stones, hard perch
and those words that linger
on the unstinging tongue.

2
The message on my answering machine:
                "I have some news" she said:
words,
    only words.
The world has a soundtrack.

        Rewind, playback: "I have some news"
Words are possibilities, long carpets rolled out.

                And again.

The world loses its soundtrack.
                    Words are
tremors the tongue makes.

3
I grew up almost convinced
that "everything has a place
and everything in its place"

but now the dead—
                I don't know
how to talk to you
since I don't know
where you are.

4
I hold pain out
like a yardstick, measure
a wound's duration,
grind my quiet teeth
on that unit, its ragged diminishment
of me.

But death is not inches,
kilometers or volumes.
It has no plot or measure, unless
someday we can count forever
on our hands.

5
Death and *breath:*
the onomatopoeia of belief:
those words with their two soft
consonants lisping
until all the pillows
are pulled abruptly away
and the words end

with a hard believing.

6
Each time I come across your names
in my phone book
I wonder about them.

Be easy if you moved — I'd draw
a line through your old address,
and I'd write a new one.

I love how children, when they
first discover their place in the world,
want it to go on
forever. Proudly they recite
                their street
                their town
                and country
                The Milky Way

                              and growing
they connect themselves to everything
that does not end. For many years everything they touch
is soft, has a name; every question an answer

and sleep comes after a story.

The Sea or Salvation

Someone in a white car speeding down
long avenues, red light flashing,
saying nothing of what somebody's knuckles hit,
and underneath them blossoms
like purple cabbage leaves.
Someone dying in smoke.
Someone's body listless with fear.
Someone reading his paper
at the breakfast table, how the words suddenly
slur and go limp.
Someone in a house full of photographs,
letters, intimate books, dying
of having nothing to remember.
Someone else dying of too much to remember.
Someone dying of cold kisses.

It's warm. It's August.
Sirens throb and wheeze down someone's street.
Vines climb the fence like trespassers.

I want to believe that less than the truth
happens all night.

I want to believe that all the sirens
are of the sea, or salvation.

2 THE GOING

"I got sawdust in my eye . . . And they said to me, 'You better go to where the eyestone is tonight.' "

. . . Both eyestones we've seen have a tiny dot—the center of a perfect whorl—and when in vinegar two or three bubbles would come out of the hole. Then it would be put in the afflicted eye. The patient must sit still or lie down while the eyestone does its work. This is simply so that it will not be lost. This is also the reason you go to the eyestone and it rarely travels.

—*Down North: The Book of Cape Breton's Magazine*

WAITING FOR THE STORM

There are days when forecast thunderstorms
are perfect, when the late afternoon
horizon is mostly fog, a vague silhouette
of hills, when tide fills the brook
that hums
what it usually croons.
                      The tide generous
bringing me things
wrapped in water.

The tide—how it wears its fullness,
how it wants to twirl the folds
of its new dress, but it's gotten fat.

And the sun tries to burn through the fog
like a parent trying to get a child's attention.
A bird whistles

another distraction and meanwhile the sky
wants to break down the door
and let itself in, wants to break open
your eyes like an oyster.

This morning herons stood
in shallow pools of eel grass and weed.
I cannot measure where
or how they stood like rocks
in a Buddhist garden.

Now each tuft of water grass
sprouts its reflection, funnels
its fireworks for minnows,
its green calligraphy.
                    I have no ink
for these brushstrokes and when the slightest
breeze changes their shape
I must try to read it all again.

THE PRINT ON THE WALL

A moment's deep island—
              find the heart
of its forest, the places
that change us
and help us understand

how the collection of old bottles
on the window ledge
is reflected in the print:
        Vue de Leutsdorf & Hammerstein
on the adjacent wall.

I remember sitting in a café, looking
out windows at angles to the street,
at reflections of people approaching,
their image in the glass like premonitions
we mistrust since they have no certainty
and may not correspond to the world.

Our landscapes are collages
we paste together with luck,
occasional resolve.

No guarantee the glue will stick.
Or that fragments, like dynasties, will fall

though sometimes we're allowed
to see how the pieces are arranged—
tinted elms beside the river bank
married now to the surreal bottles,
my favourite ones
a tender pastel.

SCRAPS

I look at watercolour-cold blue skin.
I'm reading National Geographic,
looking at the Iceman crawling,
at the crest of a mountain pass, crawling
into the twenty-first century.

I wander into the kitchen to tell
anyone who cares to know this
in this time of beautiful trivia.
Ten-year-old Amy is there, climbing,
sitting on the counter.

A German couple were hiking
in the Alps,
       I tell her,
              when they saw a head
and shoulders in the ice, thought it was a doll.

From page 36:
      He was quickly nicknamed Otzi
             after the valley north of ...

but "No, tell it like a story," Amy protests.

So I go back to the watercolour-cold blue skin,
his dirty fingernails,
his last cold breath as he leans back
to look up at the mountain, never knowing
he'd make it to my sister's kitchen.

The mountain can be the century,
a young girl's mind,
can be stories we need to tell ourselves
—larch trees blazing an orange trail—
about the Iceman's scraps
of bone needle, hazel wood,
a deerskin quiver of fourteen arrows,
a copper axe, whatever
we need to keep us going.

Skating Over the Moment

The breadth of the frozen harbour,
the archipelago of rocks enveloped
in loose pyramids of ice
that separate me from the larger
expanse: I'm waiting

for what? unable to accept
the cold here and now.

When my thoughts fly out
over these rocks, they pause,
lose some of their glide.

There are times when I feel
we are on the verge of something
astounding; we can do more
than just skate over surfaces.

But this field of ice is so still,
so inconsiderate
and perfect
it hurts:
                wind has made
a brocade of snow on the ice,
crescents of snow
that freeze one at a time,
pocket one wish
at a time.

The Book of Dreams

The dream lacks a plot, is more a sense of place and belonging, of elegant shops, a sense of listening to a quartet play hauntingly eerie Chinese music. In the dream itself I did not see London, only felt it: Covent Garden in November where there were long tables of hand-knit sweaters, textured leatherwork, Beatrix Potter mice. This is not a dream of story, but a theme of belonging and comfort, of restaurants with brass headboards and tall secluding foliage.

Dreams do have their history, but this book would be a small one, of short passages; excerpts are brief, tentative. Battles would be of a varied nature: medieval horses would ride through cobble-stoned lanes, of strangely familiar towns, on their way to something ominous, a tragedy that then lies down and sleeps like a child recovering from the flu. The horses would prance back through the streets undefeated, with the same energy as emotion. Heroes would cease to have injuries, and faces. To walk up the stairs is to walk with them, which is necessary to our dreams, the book of every night and day, of wordless dark pages you read with your eyes still or closed.

At the Centre of Things

Whenever I talk about love
I always end up staring into space;
in a crowded room, I can see
over everyone's head
and beyond
                      —there at the far end
of the room something alien sends me
to dark inner space.
                      No one notices
this creature but me
although in high school we learn words like
molecules, atoms, protons, nucleus
and love.
We're taught to believe they exist.
We're taught to believe there's
a soft truth at the centre of things
that keeps moving. Hidden in tables, chairs,
an ashtray: small lopsided mobiles
that keep rubbing their satellites on each other.
I look at surfaces, things that aren't telling
me their truth. Any minute they might start.
Any minute now I might see ...
Whenever I talk about love
I keep waiting for molecules
like little spaceships to slip up,
forsaking their equations
of density and mass.

LOOKING AT A PHOTOGRAPH OF MY PARENTS

They look back at me,
for the first time not recognising their daughter.
They wear clothes to travel in,
an unfamiliar silence.

They remind me of strangers
who people my dreams.
Where do they come from?
We are different, having dreamt them,
having such questions.

Families are accidents of blood and sequence,
collages and thick strokes.
Now we are different people
since pictures show us the bodies we are:
places we walk out of, that fill,
like our footprints, with muddy water.

In one grown child, parents can see
a family of memories:
the three-year-old running naked after his bath,
grandmother again in the arch of his eyebrows,
Uncle George in a curl of young hair.
We are different people
at different ages,
occasionally ourselves.

But they look back at me again.
Now we are different people, distances from ourselves.
Our bodies places we walk out of, landscapes
of spring. We blur our edges, soften
the hard lines of expectation
and grow into our bodies again.

THE SUN ALL DAY
    for Toni Lauriston

I remember she told me how the sun setting
is the saddest time of day.
I remember looking out the window,
waiting to see how the sun would look in my eyes,
knowing it would linger like a sadness.

And I think about the afternoon light
when I would lie on the sofa
under the windows facing west.
I would sleep under the light,
listening to songs in machines
turn until they shut off,
that click like a shadow.

Now she tells me she's ok with the sunset
but meanwhile I've grown
used to light on my eyelids,
the sofa that holds my body, lyrics
drifting through the room, my loose limbs
tired and happy, like my eyes,
from making love. I can do nothing else
but kiss him at the door when he leaves;
love is the effect of the light.

Saturdays she and I would walk to the market
downtown, past the trains under the bridge.
She'd dream of leaving town on one,
letting it take her wherever it goes.
Later we'd buy oranges,
crunchy cookies with walnuts and raisins,
and walk home with grocery bags
pulling our arms long.

So now when I think about those days,
they include her sunset, the afternoon light,
eating cookies when we get home,
my putting schoolwork off for love.

They include one of my last days in Windsor
in the spring; it was raining and cold.
I was bored walking around the house
and she sat in the living room reading
while I tried to contain the tears
I still try to explain.

And the only way I can explain them now
is with the sad light
when it seems the sun
is setting all day long.

Tubing Festival, Gaspereau

Enter at the whirlpool
where if you're drunk
you'll be seduced
by the river that swirled, sang,
pulling down that one drunk
who dove into shallow water.

So many things we cannot measure—
the river's depth, the rumour that he cracked
his skull open, the compliance
of the cows chewing grass
in the fields along the river.

Immeasurable: the crowd
in circles floated down river, trucked
back through farm fields, and so many
stars when I slept outside
on an inner tube, the stars floated
through their river.

And Gail in the evening
in tears, screaming,
screeching about how much she loves him
                  and her limbs flailed, fell
and the rest of her body falling later,
trying to catch up.

She slept it all off.
Or no, she couldn't have,
but she was quiet next morning
when we went into the whirlpool again.

FUCHSIAS LONG DISTANCE

Two cards the same,
fuchsias like court jesters in pink tights
somersaulting, sticking out their tongues.

Both birthday cards sent to me in Japan:
Christine writes she's worried about a friend's
rebound marriage,
> *sounds like you're settling in,*
alludes to my last love affair:
> *c' est la vie*
> *don' t feel too bad*
> *I don' t know what love is—*
> *emotions and shit*
and says that Bruce baked
a chocolate cake.

I think of the many plants
in her house then, and now,
green and uncomplicated.

While my grandmother
also writes of my new life:
> *It must be just grand to see*
> *many new flowers and gardens*
> *and perhaps lakes?*
of her crab-apple tree in bloom,
the tulips and lilacs soon,
of cousins visiting who I've never met,
and three beautiful fuchsias in the sun-room.
> *Hope you can decipher this*
she says promising a real letter
that never came—I didn't
expect it would:
she died a year later.

So I look at her words now,
rereading their sprawl,
thinking of the perimeters of her life
and those flowers in the sun-room
thrusting out their tongues at death.

I look at Christine's words,
how they overlap with hers,
how they, too, speak of things growing,
dying. I look at my life
in Japan that ended years ago
and at fuchsias framed by a thin ribbon
of gold, sent a distance longer
than they ever would have guessed.

THE DISHES SO SLOWLY
    for Klaus & Mary

A cold early spring day, I've taken
the train away from the city
that goes on forever growing,
the city where you can never find what
you found once on a Saturday night;
it wants to teach you its language.

I hear the city behind me
talking in the future tense

as we walk through woods,
to a temple: thatched roof, dark wood;
drive later along country roads bordered
with tall yellow grass.

But back at the house: tatami,
low tables. Preparing dinner she talks
of shiatsu, tea ceremony lessons:
    how she has to remember the words
for left hand, right hand, not to mix them
up, not to ask why or when
or where to touch the Japanese nerve.

A woman from New Jersey being taught
to be Japanese—is it possible?—
by enormous small efforts,
by taking the cup in her hand.
She deliberates each gesture,
moves in hypnotising words
of foreign instruction

and when she gets home, she tells us,
she stands in front of the kitchen sink
doing the dishes
so slowly.

THE LIGHTS BEHIND ME

Southwestern Ontario in the fall
where the unexpected happens,
relieving you of an unhappiness
that bores you. You've been in a kind of shock,
feeling you don't belong to the world,
and hoping, more than believing,
that love is a simple thing.

So why am I standing in front of a sunrise
looking down at a flat Ontario field,
as if all the sunrises I've seen
have marked their moment
and the night they came out of?

Playing Risk in a trailer in New Minas losing
track of time—we stayed up all night—
but gaining countries. When we drove home:
the sunrise over the Annapolis Valley

as if it marked all the all-night parties
of your adolescence where you're never hung over,
immune to it,
though the boys get sick outside.

But that's a long way from last night
when Rob and I went out to the country.
Every time I leave the city when I need to
I can hear the lights behind me sighing.

I didn't expect a century farmhouse
and red wine by the fire until
three or four a.m.
Restless sleep, I wondered if Rob
was coming to my bed
or not.

And then waking for the sunrise
that made the field shine.

The main thing of that day was the fields,
their new colour interrupting
the trees and their falling leaves

—the season tells on itself—

and us walking the dogs
or the dogs racing past us
so we put them in the back of the truck
when we went into town.

As if those are ordinary things
people do, not like Rob coming to my bed
hours after the sunrise
and I can't make love to him
because the body, like love, isn't so simple
when it wants someone else.
So I spend the day
doing ordinary things
that help me believe
I belong.

WHAT HE WILL TEACH US

1
We used to take the path beside the brook, but it wasn't overgrown then with alders, this path which comes out behind the hospital.

2
The room hot, a box of Kleenex by the open window—the top tissue illustrates the breeze, as Kay, half-asleep, hears me looking at her, and wakes. As sisters, we hear each other as we enter rooms. I look at her, trying to decide how she's changed. She wears a familiar night-gown, the same freckles. I've seen her with a thermometer in her mouth. I've seen her in bed with cinnamon toast, eggnog, flat ginger ale.

3
She is my little sister, I keep telling myself. I see her fighting with John. Or standing on the wharf at swimming lessons, her shorts on over her bathing suit because it is cold. Always cold for swimming lessons. Or she sits on a stool in the kitchen, a towel around her shoulders, Dad bends over her with a pair of scissors, holds them down over her wet bangs. Her eyes closed, he closes the scissors. Wet hair falls down over the towel to her shirt.

In another room her new son is sleeping, wrapped in blankets that have elephants, kangaroos in pastel pink, yellow and blue. His dark hair is wet and his hand under the flannelette moves in a dream that knows nobody's name.

4
I look at the years I've known her, at the months that shaped themselves. I've held my hand over them, felt them move inside her, but I cannot know them, as she tries to decide why I look at her like this.

5
A nurse enters with the child asleep, flannelette tight around him. The more I look at his face the more he is himself. I imagine he's looking at us, searching us for parts of our selves we share. He doesn't need words for this; they are deep inside him, and already he knows who he is. It is us he is having to learn, and he will find us in the way he turns in his sleep, the way he feels the blanket for the silk. He teaches us to tell him who we are before him.

6
I fear him, unsure if I will ever know him, but he is gentle with this, sleeps never knowing what I sing. What lullaby? A plaintive tune that cries in the dark. Inside he is sleeping, inside the song. She pulls her night-gown up over her milk-swollen breast. She is both the years behind her and the years ahead. The window is open. The top tissue in the Kleenex box is still. All my thinking has calmed the breeze, the room so close. And hot.

THE CAREFUL PATH BACK TO NAÏVE

We had just passed the place
where the inlet narrows
before it widens, where islands
hold the opposite shore
behind their backs like children
with fistfuls of daisies.

We were on our way to the beach
when we hardly saw it,
							a cat ...?
... no time to brake.

The kids oblivious in the back seat
eager to jump over waves.

While the two of us in the front seat
after that split second holding—
							her eyes said
							say nothing—the children ...

As if the lie would wrap the animal,
close its eyes. We were holding
to all the possibilities,
to what we couldn't bring ourselves
to say about injury,
how an animal dies,
why some go on living
in pain, why sometimes life
is something caught in the throat.

The two of us reeling.
The kids uncomprehending,
if we told them
hearing *cat*   thinking *home,*   thinking *safe.*

We couldn't picture
trying to find the cat's owner:
walking up a driveway
to find a young girl behind a screen door
looking at us, waiting for us
to say the special password.

                      Pleeease
               we would say   *let us in ...*

What the beach would have been
after all that: a letting go,
our taking more than a few steps
forward and back, the waves
pouring up the sand with a strange
new urgency,
the kids jumping in them
but not with the same buoyancy and ease.

Their slight delay, as if they keep turning
to us   *but?*
as if they place their hands on either side
of your face and once they hold you realise
they have nothing to say.

ISLAND GOING

As children we'd go out to the island,
to the point where the inlet empties
into the harbour, where boats sail back
and forth through the day,
back to the inlet at nightfall,
mosquitoes returning
to the porch light.

We'd go out to the rocks painted red
for the treasure we hoped to find,
would crawl up the tallest rock,
to its mast and cry *All's Well*
like boys in paintings by Winslow Homer
as boats sailed by.

Who names the weeds of the sea?

Now I go out to the island alone
to walk along the shore, to look
at the other side of memories
as if the tide washes and cleans them.

We also picked berries from a bush,
weren't supposed to eat them;
we rolled them in our hand till they burst—
blood blisters on our fingertips.

Nothing was perfect, but even weeds
will flower—sand flies dance
under the rags of the sea.
By the shore, I jump from rock
to rock, find a footing, balance
because that's all we can do.

THE BLUE EGG
>	*Nobody advertises slow miracles.*
>	—Donna Williams

Not the nests of Easter
with its chocolate eggs
wrapped in green and pink foil,
but the nests you find in trees,
the quiet miracle of the bird
flying in with another thread—
                    hushaby, lullaby
of swallows, sparrows, gold
finches and wrens—
no advertisement for blatancy,
but for wait and maybe
you'll see. To live
by discretion and caution
is the law of the woodland and thicket.

But what of the blue egg
I found on the driveway?
Cupped it in my palm,
to feel the throb of the bird-to-be
as I look up, to the tree branches
for answers. What fears
disturbed the nest?

A boy, primary to grade nine,
is sent off to school, his homework
undone and the words—meaningless,
something he cobbles together
from friends, his older sister
who brings A's home
that get heaped on the fridge
till they fall
out of a dusty mess.

Years later the boy will marry,
have a child. The day she is born
he cups in his hands
the pink soles of her feet.
After too many grades of discretion
he promises himself
he will read to her many stories.

And when words fall sometimes
from his grasp he will say
them slowly. When he finds a blue egg
under a tree, he will tell his daughter
how they came to be there.

When We Turn Around

What's summer without fireworks?
The day goes down
like a child's top coming out
of its spinning, spinning.
You ease into evening's slower motion,
turn around to find the sunset
pouring strawberry wine over the city's horizon
as if to toast the doors quietly opening and closing,
the people who pour out of them filling the streets.
Who, like bumblebees milling around a red flower,
so eagerly traipse up the hill
as if they will inherit the sky by their effort.

Some are already camped out on the grass,
on the hill sloping towards the harbour.
A city of children—we are all younger

under summer's holiday thunder and spark,
under houseplants of starlight that wilts,
melts down into star dust and powder,
golden spiders, a night garden
of flaming wild flowers.

But when I turn around again
it's mid-morning; I'm in a coffee shop
when I see them, two people talking,
but not talking, signing.

Oh, the dance of their hands
playing the harp of the open air,
the touch-and-go of fingertips
that dart about like swallows,
like bats suddenly
in the breath-taking blue of the twilight.

I remember looking at a photograph
of my lover's hand light on my arm,
feeling the electricity of his touch.

For these hands I could go deaf,
move differently in the world
and shape fireworks
that spill off the paisley swirls
of fingerprints, little maps marking
the elevation of mountains silent and new.

Rooms for Yourself

You should start with shawls, throw carpets
of moss pulled off rocks and the musty earthen floor.
Trees would be your four corners,
their limbs bent down would make a door.

The country has its quiet assignments.

Then keep to your course, find the barn
by the roadside, the barn like an old woman
remembering her children.

Bales of hay, echoes of the ancient smells
of animals, the dry grain of barn board.
Have you found the boxes that didn't make it
to the attic? Of thick postcards cobwebbed with words.
History wears a long skirt and climbs
steps to board a train, its compartments garnished
with wine velvet, silver, cut glass.

Did you read the words aloud to each other
as we did, imagining cities of people
on these fields? Or in the woods where
birches and poplar turn
sheds and more barns to the angle
where they disappear?

Don't tiptoe in like fairy-tale children,
don't slow-walk back to these rooms
closer to the earth than we were,
our breath caught on branches, fallen leaves
around a rusted can.

But go boldly back to the heap
of weathered boards. You won't break
like the bottles you want to find intact
under the wood. Dream of windowsills of glass
against glass, light entering their stories.
Go now.

THE PHOTOGRAPHER
> *they've passed their test in life*
> —Diane Arbus

At night when she blooms, she enters
her dark-room charged with discovery,
the seduction of the image she bathes
in solutions she loves
for their lack of remorse.

Or she goes out into those late
and early hours in the Bronx
or the Bowery, rides the subway
out to Coney Island, hunting
for the private faces
of those aristocrats of the night
who were born with their trauma.

Take me with you, Diane,
when, heart pounding, you spend the night
with the man who calls himself
the Sage of the Wilderness
and the blind giant whose dog
howled at the moon.

Teach me, Diane, to live with that dread
that one day we will be tested.
The earth will heave up, topple
our houses which will burn.
Mountains too will flame
and thunder will break
down the nerves and cells of the body.

When the flash goes off
we are stunned, wondering if darkness
will rearrange itself like the pigeons
scurrying from the ledge
of Moondog's hotel, like you
who courts awkwardness
as it helps us unlearn our disguises.

Maybe I should stand
on a windy New York street
and rearrange myself for the lesson.

Help me climb down the ladder
of respectability,
the ladder that's made of rope
and we'll throw ourselves in the air,
into the circus act without
glitter and spangles.
That's how I'll learn disorder, impact
and how to fall.

3 THE EYESTONE

When there is someone to be helped the eyestone is taken out of sugar and carefully cleaned. John A. said that down North it would be put in a weak vinegar solution.

"I was sawing wood at Bay St. Lawrence. I got sawdust in my eye . . . And they said to me, 'You better go to where the eyestone is tonight.' I went and they put me to bed with it. Put it in my eye. And you couldn't notice it. The size of it, you'd think it would bother you—but it didn't. I woke up and my eyes were clear. I was twenty-two or twenty-four years old."

. . . In the eye, the eyestone would move round and round the eyeball searching for the speck, and the eye would be clear and the eyestone would be returned to the sugar.

—*Down North: The Book of Cape Breton's Magazine*

THE DAY YOU SAW THE WORLD

Where the houses end
water begins,
narrows
and widens
eventually going out to sea.

The houses end.
The world begins to open up;
     you're lightened
by the sparseness
of low tide, the water
seeping in around eel grass.

The world begins
to reveal ... begins to be more
than its usual self:
     it's taken off
some of its clothes to sun
itself on the sand.

For the first time you see the world
is a mermaid who's not afraid
of nakedness, the simplicity of skin.
When you lie down beside her
she will confess something
of her other faces, her lovers
and wounds, how many times
she was caught
in a fine net and how she managed
to swim away.
She is more agile than we know.

    And more loving.
When you lie down her kisses
are the waves
making way, pulling sand
around your ankles.

You will lie with her
a long time. Sometimes to love this world
you have to let her help you.

When you wake your skin will be flushed
and when you put your clothes back on
reluctantly you'll find sand
in your pockets.

THE AUCTION

The trees like old phonographs
scratch their needles on the day
winding down, bid
farewell with a chorus of good night,
good night, goodbye.

        Green they were—going once,
        darker to black—going twice
        and gone.

Sold to evening that keeps
track of the stocks
and green bonds of the earth.

Evening that can't outbid night, the darkening sky,
the constellations, the old carousel
of animals that roar and prance.
Their solid flanks in need of paint,
their tails that need to be tightened

before morning buffs,
polishes and auctions off
the sky's antiques.

MORNINGS BY THE WATER
for Leslie

1
The first morning the alarm goes off
in the midst of a vague dream: something
about wings, about seaweed and water
you want to make exact
but you have to get up,
make the kids their lunches
and light the stove to warm the cold kitchen.
Outside wind shapes distant whitecaps.

You dress quickly
under the low ceiling,
and in the kitchen, fill the stove,
burning yourself—the faded scar
on your arm later will be a birthmark.

The next morning is different:
you wake before the alarm,
lie in bed for awhile
looking out the window at the calm harbour.
Sun. A pale blue sky.
Yesterday's damp wind
has moved out to sea.
During the day three herons
settle at the end of an island.

In pools of seaweed they stand motionless,
their grey wings telling me
I was born by the water,
my mother a blue heron
and those are my sisters out there.
The water is calm
and my family increases.

2
The herons are flying
down to the water
where reflections aren't simple things.
The water, as fragile as morning,
has to wait for dream-stillness. Then,
as less than an afterthought,
the herons unfold their wings.

Again

> *I need to sleep on [that poem] five hundred times.*
> —Donald Hall, *The Language of Life*

And I dream it in different parts
of my dream-machine, sleep on
five hundred beds until I find the one that fits
perfectly, though I toss
and fight with it: pull hair, kick shins, slap
its face that looks so much
like my own.

We squabble about names
and what it wants to call me—
distracted, dreamy, and poor, until

demons become dragonflies,
mayflies who live but a day
or two with their transparent wings.
Oh, to eavesdrop on angels.

Sometimes I'm not sure what I do—
I daydream, mull over
its insubstantiality, can hear
wings speeding off, zigzagging
toward what heaven?

as I debate the true names
of the real and the mythical,
the body and wing, their wondrous detail

where what will pass
is the whole zoo, the whole kit
and crazy caboodle—that phrase
may open another dream—

and what will pass
this way once
is worth it
though it may never come again.

I WANT TO INTERVIEW ANGELS

I want to meet all the angels
and bandage their scratches and wounds.
I want to interview them, ask them
their middle names, their true genealogies;
want to look them in the eye,
at the worldly and extraordinary colours there.

I want to pick their brains,
to write the real biographies of the ones who bruise
and limp into the bad sections of town; angels live there,
I'm sure, on low incomes with their hearts
locked inside their mortality.

I want to know how angels age and cry,
how they heal their sick and dying.

> We feel angels
> as wings inside us,
> as a muscle twitch,
> a heart murmuring
> or burned.

Or we don't feel them at all.
They concentrate on potions, charms,
cats in the appropriate neighbourhood.
They read recovery books, philosophy,
feminism, the book yet-to-be-written
on the government of the spirit; they read
between the lines, rhyme and scan
the blank spaces, fix us in reverie
to objects that hold our gaze until
—fingers snap—and we pull
at solutions, like scarves,
if we are lucky, that no longer darken our eyes.

THE HAND-MIRROR

It was solid, medieval,
in a dream insubstantial now
as warm weather we long for
during the winter.

It was not wooden or silver
engraved with initials,
but gray stoneware flecked,
seeded with mica and other minerals.
There was a wide circumference
around the empty glass—why
could I not see myself?
Its sturdy handle
was notched like a key
but softer
so that I could place my fingers
around its undulations.

The mirror, still empty and clear, was heavy
but not as ponderous as the days and nights
from which it had appeared.

                      But when I turned the mirror
                      on its edge!
     —like our understanding of the world
not meant to be laid flat or bare

not meant to judge us fair or more fancy—
when I held it at an angle,
away from my face,
its grayness turned lustrous,
to royal blues, hummingbird green,
colours
        that spilled, like holograms,
                and danced,
              and reflected
the wealth of the world.

THE DAY THE BOOKMOBILE CAME

It always parked in Bettyann's driveway.
I remember reaching up, placing
one foot on the step;
how the metal rang faintly.

With the next foot, I was off the ground,
leaving a summer's day
        and our secret field,
to step into a room
full of books!

I remember how dark it was inside
and quiet—I heard the rustle
of pages, the quick intake of breath
when someone found
a particular surprise, a hushed reverie
I did not associate with these women,
our mothers, searching the shelves.

I remember how we went
straight to the back of the long room
to find the books that fit
the palm of our hands.

And later brought them
to the desk, my looking up, watching
the pages fan open, the books
paper accordions, their song
                tangible
as they were so efficiently,
so assuredly stamped.

I remember, too, how I thought the librarian
and driver must be married, living
and working side by side in this enclosed world.

I imagined them at night,
parked in someone's driveway,
pulling down the bed they hid
and because it was already made,
they climbed into it
with their clothes on
so they'd be ready for us
in the morning.

AFTER READING "COLLECTED LANDSCAPES"
for Roo Borson

And then I came to *the brain's pink canyons*
so familiar I could imagine the exact angle
of descent, as if already
I had looked down into them,
had seen the rivers below
walking away into exclamations
—every drop of water has its moment.

Pathways of little vegetation,
of few words
and even fewer passersby—
the chance Anasazi out of the corner
of your eye and fossils surrendering a silence,
a name on the tip of your tongue.

          So much is repeated;
I thought I walked off
an edge of the world,
stood on the air like a cartoon character
whose ignorance keeps him there,
me in mid-air waiting
for more detail,
for every small thing
to explain us.

Reading in the Bath

Washed once with water,
I'm washed a second time with words,
their heat and liquid

coursing through me. Poems moving
like waterfalls whose lace
drops its thunder through us.

Is it because we are mostly water
that the poem rhymes us? I wake dreaming
things that float away, call them back

in the water as I read
rivers in the country of our bodies.
Some meandering through farm fields,

their quiet harvests.
Others rivers deliberately slow
and lovely for it, in places

where heat deliberates and floats.
Remember the day it was so hot in the city
we went out to Lawrencetown beach,

where wind pushed waves into paisleys
grey with cold cold fog?
We huddled for that poem,

slapped our arms warmer,
lay down on the sand to feel
where warmth and water had been.

Remember the summer night—the night read
to us, calling us and we went
out to the lake after dark,

took off our clothes
on impulse, on the pulse of the poem,
the lake, that night, the lake water

lapping us up. And more summer water,
earlier we explored creeks, every possible
beginning of water

because it was water.

At the Rapids

Can you hear the corn growing?
A man writes a letter to a radio
talk show host, saying
                I was curious,
                wanted to know ...

During the evening goes out
to lie between the stalks,
at the kitchen table
next morning writes,
                Yes you can hear it—in places
like Iowa
where it grows six inches
overnight.

Why would anyone not believe him?
Think of corn silk
like stockings,
and husks bursting open,
comet tails and fireworks
that wither and close
come morning.

And can't you hear yourself
growing—close your eyes,
push your ears closed
and you'll hear inside
the current at the rapids.

LEGEND

The calm water teases.
A cormorant stands guard
on the tall rock at the end of the spit.

Sometimes looking out at the water
I see something pushing up
from under the surface.
The first drops of water rise
and pull, easing it through—

the long neck of a sea serpent,
a priestess dressed in seaweed robes,
or an arm holding a sword or a key.

But the water teases, unperturbed.
To look out at the water and find nothing
but the cormorant spreading his heraldic wings.
To live this close to belief
that we will be witness
is to find the tide a full bowl
and brimming,
a seagull sailing
its accurate rim.

Gratitude, from the Clam Factory

Brought to the wood's edge by glaciers
rocks here held their breath,
puffed out their large cheeks
so they would not be forever
submerged.

Rocks taller than me, than the old scouts
of the trees on Indian Island.
Bleached clam shells gravel the factory driveway.
We watch ice cakes slap the whitecaps
                                    and sail forth
and by the shoreline smaller cakes
buoyed by frozen seaweed-anchors
and rocks. We can almost pattern the harbour's
sandbars; the currents send
the ice one way
and then another.

A month later the harbour is ice-free,
the only trace of winter the cold wind
that comes off the water, the wind
that skirts down to catch a ride on ice boats
but in disappointment lifts up
its cold air and takes off.

A wind always looking for surfaces
and craft. What little my life
could have been, what I might
never have reached.

ON THE PATH TO THE WATERFALL
  in memory of Raymond Carver

I close a book and open
another, and in doing so
have found someone to kiss.
Just as one man grew up kissing books and bread
so I kiss you now on paper
because ...   Why do I do this?

"I've always squandered" you said, always
immersed yourself in the liquid present.

     Sept. '87, spitting up blood
     early March, brain tumour
     and early June, more tumours in the lungs

after seven weeks of machines
making your mind glow fluorescent
as the full moon on a clear night.

Do writers have an easier time
believing in the future? That they can rewrite
endings? Chekhov kept reading train schedules
away from the town of his death. Your list:
                    peanut butter
               eggs ...
          Australia?
            Antarctica?

Your poems "like traffic accidents,
or miraculous escapes," someone said. You, who wrote
"When hope is gone, the ultimate sanity is to grasp at straws."
The eleventh book is not a miraculous escape. It's a new
path to the waterfall.

So I kiss you on paper,
my eyes kissing words.

       Recently, talking to my seven-year-old niece
       on the location of the soul:
                " Where is it?" I asked.
       She did not hesitate, but leaned over
       and with one hand touched the bottom of her foot.

Early June, news of tumours in your lungs,
you find poetry in Chekhov's prose
and he steps forward, train tickets in his hand,
as if he is sending you to those places
where there's something else
inside everything: words inside words and poetry
in prose, all without trespasses.

Do the dying discover this
transparency, life losing
its solidity?   "I'm travelling faster" you said.

You wrote "Gravy"
about how you quit drinking after
you were told you had six months to live.
Every minute after that unforgettable
and ten loving years more
than what you bargained for.

What you bargained for!
Tess and you sitting on the deck facing
the Strait of Juan de Fuca,
marvelling at what you were allowed,
on a day, I imagine, when each wave
has its own waterfall.

How we can plagiarise, lift whole passages
like Tchaikovsky who took Beethoven's music
as his own and said   "I have a right. I love him."
I kiss your words.
Love's audacity is huge.

* * *

And because the choices we make
survey the past as well as the present,
so Alexander in Persia opened the Iliad
after he had given himself over to grief.

"He even promised to give up wine" you wrote,
a statement that turns its head
to look at the promises you made
years before, when everything was gravy.

You knew you were blessed. Each morning
you stood in front of the painting
of salmon who fight their way upstream.
Their blue ferocity is yours,
and ours too, I suppose, but you make it
look easy.

Your father's wired smile
at death saying
> *Don't worry, it's not*
> *as bad as it looks.*

You later, carrying your suit home
from the cleaners, tearing the plastic,
reaching through to the other side.

The waterfall is like that too: each drop
of water:

> *Make use of the things around you*
> *...*
> *Put it all in,*
> *Make use.*

So this is why I kiss you,
your words, those words
that lead to deeds and prepare the soul:
because I try so hard to use everything,
because I might drop a book or a piece of bread,
might drop your words and the bread
that fed your necessities.
This then, by way of apology
for what might, in future, fall to the floor
and for the future itself.